As If Words

As If Words

poems

Jeanne Lohmann

2012 · Fithian Press, McKinleyville, California

Published by Fithian Press
A division of Daniel and Daniel, Publishers, Inc.
Post Office Box 2790
McKinleyville, CA 95519
www.danielpublishing.com

Distributed by SCB Distributors (800) 729-6423

LIBRARY OF CONGRESS CATALOGING-IN-PUBLICATION DATA
Lohmann, Jeanne.
 As if words : poems / by Jeanne Lohmann.
   p. cm.
 ISBN 978-1-56474-522-4 (pbk. : alk. paper)
 I. Title.
 PS3562.O463A93 2012
 811'.54--dc23
          2011034234

We need, in love, to practice only this:
letting each other go. For holding on
comes easily; we do not need to learn it.

—Rainer Maria Rilke,
"Requiem"

Contents

Part Three: Wet Weather

Part Four: His Body in the World

Part Five: Living Alone

Part One

Making Angels in Chicago

For New Lovers in North Country

You will not be alone here. You will find others
and greet them, lovers out of time and long ago honeymoons
on these border lakes: Gunflint, Seagull, Saganaga, Basswood,
Namakan. Say the names and they turn to music the dead will hear
and sing back to you. Be attentive when you pass on the portages.
Follow their trails, as the voyageurs followed the trail of moose
and caribou. Lift your paddles to hail them as you come round
islands of stone and alder and blueberry, or make your way
across the muskeg. Look for canoes on the gleaming water,
the straight-backed men and women bending and stroking
or resting and riding with the current. You will find them,
the lovers here before you, find their names on old portage signs
nailed to the trees. If you don't see the names, be easy.
The lovers are here. The beaver have seen them, the great pike
in the black waters know they are here. The heron that watches you
watches them running the rapids not far ahead. Their voices
echo around you in the cries of the loon.

If white and yellow water lilies still bloom in these lakes,
cut one and fix it in your hair. Breathe that fragrance
with your kisses. On stormy nights lie together in your tent,
listen to rain on your overturned canoe. Listen to your hearts
that are safe as the packs stowed under the gunwales, your matches
dry for new fire, the map folded in its case. If the trails
are poorly marked, no matter, you will find a way through
tamarack and birch, come tired and breathless to the next
blue lake. They are good company, the lovers who sat in the sun
on these same high rocks and tossed crumbs at persistent jays.
Take pictures of yourselves naked and solitary in this wilderness,
come home with the taste of blueberry that never leaves your mouths.

When You Say My Name

Safe in your mouth,
my name is sleeping.

Because you love me
my name is yours

to say as no one else
can say it. How is it

your voice knows
so secret a way to caress

the syllables, and then
give them like small birds

to the air, where they
go on flying, and singing?

Yes, there is

a making-love bird that lives in the throat
and calls in the mating time
with a small pure note of catch-at-the-breath
to the rising beat of its wings
                              O
then   *O*
      O
no singer can match
and a hushdown dying

        sweet
                sweet
                        sweet

Making Angels in Chicago

Midnight. The wind easy at last,
thick snow falling.

New-married we
dress and go outdoors
where each thing is
given its own comforter, the world
bedding down in its beauty. We run
back to the place we grow young in
blue frozen nights
we remember.

Filling our hands with snow, we throw it
high toward the window. *You friends asleep,*
wake up! Come and see! It will not
look this way tomorrow, or even
one minute from now.

But I have forgotten
whether you joined us, or only
opened your window.

What stays are angels
we made on the neighbors' lawns,
how we lay down in snowfall streets
opening our arms and singing hallelujah.
For a while there was heaven
cold on our necks. The wet stars
rained in our faces, the air
piercing and pure as if spring
already were here.

When we rose from the ground
we saw the shapes we had been,
the snow
filling our wings with feathers.

Long Day, and the Child Asleep

A lump in dough, the child
asleep under the sheets
and the mounded covers
does not move.

Our arms remember
that sudden shift in weight,
how heavy the body
when sleep claims it,

each part of the long day
multiplied in the flesh
and the small bones
as freight for the breath to carry,

absolute surrender
to the soft and yeasty dark
where dreams rise and rest,
rise again.

Quartet

Firstborn Son
for Steve

There is that place where the seas
divide, and man walks through.
Someone said the first step is
how the waters part, the opening
of the passage.

Separate from us, insular,
you walk worlds of music and mountains,
climbing the coastal ridges
where wind shortens the grass
and ice-plant holds the hills.
It flowers in sand and salty air.

Sundust keeps you steady
where the long trails go. We
share this certainty: no return.
Together we know what never can be taken.

Your private demons,
your singular angels
know where the blessing is
hidden. They keep the holy ground.

Our arms stay open.
Walk through them. Sing
the shining stone under time,
and the water falling.

Poem for David

There was new light snow
in early October,
a damp edge to the wind.
Earth expected some arrival.
You came, hungry and laughing,
pushing your way to life,
needing no one's assistance.
Awake in the joyful dark
we sang our separate praises.

You merry, warm-hearted little boy,
maker of mud pies, tunnel-digger,
taker of dangerous chances,
collector of toy machines,
keeper of the family zoo,
enthusiast, tester of limits,
helper in the tight times,
clear eyes wide to the world,
asking friendlier tomorrows.

Our pride in you grows faster
than all your running years.
Though we have hurt one another,
love began this adventure
and stays constant, a voice
for saying, now, and aloud,
the secret gifts we have treasured.
Turn them over in your heart:

We have watched you dance,
we have marked your grace
and your grave courtesy,
the way you warm cool places
with your laughter,
your helpfulness to friends.
We have noted the strong curve
of your shoulder, hands shaping clay
on the spinning potter's wheel.

Life takes the shape you give it,
whirling the substance to order,
fingers firm on the forms,
cutting away surplus,
heat hardening the glazes.
Finding, making what you want,
your colors run true as the earth.
We rejoice in all that you are.

Mother to Daughter
for Karen

moon-child, elfin-wild,
squirrel in the snow,
woods-lover, pagan daughter
hanging mistletoe

earth-flower, gypsy-free
smiling in your dreams
tendril-reacher, ancient teacher
moving with the streams

song-bringer, trick-springer
climbing up the stars
feast-maker, wonder-waker
leaning on the bars

gift-bearer, beauty-wearer
strong-handed friend
web-spinner, joy-winner
happiness to spend

sea-wisher, golden fisher
sifting through the sand
foam-blower, salt-knower
take life in your hand

plant-grower, seed-sower
rain dancer, sunlit answer

Sixteenth Birthday Poem
for Brian

You grow tall so quickly
brown-gold bearded boy
long-legged life-strider,
man in the making.

Lover of tales and legends,
magician of many parts,
you hunt your own.
Riding sound-waves to visions
you grow your own rhythms.

Your possibles are starbursts.
You pause at their centers,
all things promises.

Look over your shoulder,
you'll find him,
that clever imp
snuggling under the rainbow,
winsome blond boy
last of our sproutings,
quicksilver puddle-glum son.

Keeper of secrets,
riddle the gentle surprise
of your smile.

Paean For My Man

My man has a bristling golden beard
that springs and curls to my fingertips,
lines of laughter grow at his eyes
and gentleness plays on the curve of his lips.

My man's mind is a darting bird,
with joy I follow its travels.
From bough to branch of evergreen
the singing moves, and the skein unravels.

My man's hands are mystery.
Strong and free in a tangent wonder,
they open the gates to music and sleep,
they waken tides and the thunder.

My man's body is taut and clean,
fresh from windy air and the sun.
We fit together and dance delight
when loving makes our bodies one.

The Best Part of a Day in Florence

We walk through history, marvel
at paintings and frescoes, bridges,
churches, and come at last to *Casa Guidi*
on *Via di San Felice a Ema,* house where
the Brownings lived and loved,
where Elizabeth died in Robert's arms.

The house is *in restauro,* and people say
there isn't much to see. We stand
across the street, remember the poets' words
and work, their tender story.
Oblivious to passersby, I hold your hand
and say the sonnet: "How do I love thee?"
I never say it truer, counting the ways.

You take me in your arms and kiss me
then and there, on that street in Florence
in front of *Casa Guidi.* We smile to think perhaps
the long-dead lovers see. We want them to know.

How Could You Not

remember the road to Belvedere,
the cloistered sisters behind the stone wall,
the house of friends with an outdoor shower
where your man in love made sacrament
of soap and water, sang *cantabile* to his Maker,
glad for the body he was glad to be in,
thankful for skin and hair, each pore,
and the shining bubbles streaming off,

remember the white towel slapped across his back,
a brisk rubdown between the legs, attention
he gave to balls and cock, each perfectly jointed toe
and finger, his face and neck and ears,
how then, wet towel over his shoulders
he came indoors clean and singing *Ave*
for joy under the wide and open sky,
the cathedral of the world?

Choosing Sculptures in the Boboli Gardens

This morning two photographs return me to Italy's
summer paradise and playground, bring me smiling
up from dreams, to find you embracing the young
marble body of some unknown Roman goddess.
Your one arm's around her waist, hand on her solid hip,
the devil in your eyes as you play a winsome Puck
for the camera.

Since my god is poetry, I choose a flying Pegasus
astride the air, nostrils flaring, carved tail flowing
in the imagined wind. High on his massive pedestal,
one grounded hoof is all I can reach to touch.
Dwarfed by the god, I stand there, hopeful.

But your photo, Love, is the one I much prefer,
your impish face inviting me to share your Eros secret,
as if there's new fun waiting for us in bright Italian sun,
and for our playful bodies after dark.

Sidewalk Café

Late August in the evening light
Zurich found a mildness now
it was closing time. Theaters
were out, the traffic gone.
The waiters knew their work
was nearly done, and greeted us
with less than grace,
though expert charm stayed easy,
almost warm. This final night
we had no need of wine,
but weary and at ease
were quite content, and watched
how light reflected from the stone.

Tomorrow's flight would take us home.
We'd walked these foreign cobbled streets
the length of summer long, and here
our talk was full of all the day
had been, presents we had found,
and suitcase room for packing them,
our children we would see. Your hand
was on my own. Familiar quiet settled down.

Two women near us rose to leave,
and stopping by our table, asked
if they might interrupt to tell
how seeing us, they paused.
They came, they said, to praise
the ways we looked our love, some joy
we might not know shone through.
For this our language had no words.
We thanked these strangers for their gift,
and smiled. All that we knew
we could not ever say.

Part Two

Of Marriages and Mountains

Summer, San Francisco

Wind surfs all night in the canyons
between condos, office buildings,
flattens the cineraria, breaks down
the Nile lilies, black spot
afflicts the roses, pigweed
rooting in the beds.

Summer's skewed and in retreat
that used to lie lazy and sweet
in Mid-West July, when we
stretched out long in the grass.

Who diluted the lemonade?
Who cut the hammock from the trees?

Fog slides under doors,
penetrates jackets, sweaters
clean to the bone,
hangs on.

From sea and harbor, the horns
celebrate *basso profundo.*

At Ocean Beach, blowing sand
scrapes summer off the skin,
cancels the calendar,
pursues us to the car.

Sail-surfers coast into gray water,
go under and rise
over and over,
farther out than I want anyone to be.

I Never Was a Wary One

I never was a wary one
and only lately have begun
the gentle art of perfidy.

Now you share the secret prize
you carry dark behind your eyes,
I wear a mask of enmity.

It is not love you give away,
but candor goes. In disarray
my life turns toward duplicity.

There's mischief here you do not know
who lay aside our treasure so:
the single heart. Simplicity.

The Truth Is

a tethered horse, my darling
makes everybody nervous

the animal wants out whether he
looks docile under leather or
paws at the ground

when fine muscles quiver and
great eyes send messages
something has to give

it's running keeps them fit
they say, night comes
they want their oats again

put an ear close to earth
you hear thunder,
horses on the loose

tramping down the salt grasses,
breaking up the heartland

Blues For Middle Age

They grow
    apart.

She listens,
    and she thinks he
    does not love her.

She dreams of that best kiss
    ever. Furious,
    she starves away.

All the signs say
    Keep Out.

He hides his dreams
    and writes them down
    in shorthand.

His silences are longer
    than usual.

He carries suitcases
    for other women.

It's hard keeping his eye
    on the road.

They hoped for better things—
    fire, perhaps,

the comfort of time
    opening.

Shell Beach

There was a day she would not choose to keep
remembering how long he looked at young
bronzed women on the sand. His eyes were deep
evasions of her own. The shallow tide ran strong

where all things moved to grace the swimmers' day.
The seagulls soared and shone in light that held
so close its warm bright fierceness kept away
the shadow, cold beneath the perfect shell

he stumbled over, then dropped into her hand.
When it was time to go they left the beach
and climbed a path that led across the stone.
There was an open space she hoped to reach.

Clear in the light she walked ahead of him.
He watched the drops of water run and break
on her bare back. His eyes returned again
where invitation was, and did not speak.

She smiled to find the summer trees were where
they'd been, and put the towel inside the ring
of logs. Her welcome met his backward stare.
Her body tightened to a changing thing

he would not want. Too many thoughts were true,
and disappearing light was only one.
Her fingers caught upon the shell and knew
the shape of coldness going from the sun.

What I Need to Hear

No. Do not say good-bye.

    Say you will miss me.
    Say there will be some
        absence.

A fallen red camellia on the stairs.

    Say you will pick it up, and find
    a fire that burns your hand.

Jealous Woman Weaving

She makes his garments as she may,
covers him from head to toe,
in the fabric of their days
sets designs that lovers know.
Her pattern deftly fixed upon him
marks the time when he will go

abroad in all the charming world,
across the daily thoroughfare
where danger's in a curving motion,
in other legs and long bright hair,
siren loveliness to lure him,
tempting fancies everywhere.

She calls fine magic into play
when he goes free, a handsome man
for wandering loose in company
with snares beside on either hand.
With firm delight and silken thread
she weaves his skin as best she can.

From the Shore

I watched the big wave coming.
You were out so far, and
took it sideways,
going under.

Water held you
preserved in green,
a specimen in glass,
your body tumbling
like those stones
the jewelers polish. Then
the curving broke, let go,
and with you,
all the water fell.

2.

The big wave in "Kanagawa-oki,"
one of Hokusai's *Thirty-Six Views of Mt. Fuji,*
has fingers clawed into lace,
water reaching like arms,
poured into shapes like some old
shrouded genius of the sea.
Fisher boats ride under the arch,
they sail behind and in,
before the trough.

Froth bubbles hang in air and never fall,
as Hokusai's wave does not fall and is
always falling. Everything in that picture
bends and curves, holds and is held. Fuji
stays serene, showered by drops that stop
short of the mountain's cone.

There are waves behind this one,
more water
coming on.

On Saving the World

You have a world to save, my sweet;
I want to salvage me.
Your causes are magnificent;
my need is charity.

Your concerns range far and wide,
love seems a narrow door.
Is there some quiet meeting-ground
where we have been before?

Well-met our worlds if joined to find
in mercy of this place
a universe which moves but holds,
and keeps the centered space.

Love Asks for Centering

The concentrate dilutes to thinner potion,
edges blur to kindness, and the heart
in hazard to peripheral motion
hunts hidden center where love's art
shapes bright and hot a lucid passion
of braver stuff than wanting not to hurt.
This goodness is no satisfying ration
when all our need is firmer meat.
Fuzzy fringes will not seal the weight
of juice in ripening heavy fruit.

Then turn from guilt too late remembering,
speak burning core love feeds upon,
or say no word at all. Dismembering
the whole, uncertain word by word, is stone
that smothers fire and splinters hope,
bending the axis till the tipping world
grows perilous. Lines slide across the map,
the moving lands collide. What directions hold?
The heart requires a center that secures
its faith, the steady passion that endures.

Of Marriages and Mountains

Some hands that hold on heights let go
for sharper steeper downward slide.
What heart could be committed, pure,
when distant viewpoints call delight?
Who would test the crevices of dark
in mountains rough, rewarding, sure?

The ranges hold together. Elements
of earth, rock, air fuse into mountains
where twisting trails descend and rise.
It takes the thrust of inwardness
to shape this mass on which we climb.
That moving force determines weight and size.

True marriage is a mountain, no mistake,
heartland that's elevated, absolute,
and makes demands. Quick walking will not do.
The intricate solidity of mass and peak
requires some narrow places, folds of stone.
The hands that hold help one another through.

In Opposition

We hurt and are hurt
And have each other for healing.
It is healing. It is never whole.
　　　*—Wendell Berry, "Marriage" (*Collected Poems*)*

I cannot put my loving you on call,
in cage, well-groomed, content to wait
for times you choose to come, and let
the creature loose for daily walks and air.
This is no docile pet to call for romp
or chase the sticks, or follow where you will.
My loving you is more than animal
and cannot walk obedient by your side,
be mirror to your need, or glove to pride.

Nor will I make a chain of words
as amulet to keep the hurt away.
When love and freedom cross and disagree
no magic comes to ease the strain.
Then I set out to find a place of trust
that guards and keepers never know,
where tears are safe, and anger right to flow.
But that the work is easy, no one claims.
It asks a harder thing than cage or chains.

Passage

Let our swords grow words
and hands be haven.
Plant kisses berry wild.
Hold harbor arms.
Too long in the wind's eye
and the craft founders.
If we turn enemy
the city falls.
These are thicket times.
Let us tend to the clearing
of the old thorn hedges.
Light knows the way.
I love you is passage
under the spines.

After Wine Tasting, the Napa Valley

we drink vintage memory
this marriage ages well

our bodies pour one into another
the full glasses shine

Naming the Birds

To find a voice for love
is a way
of loving.
　　　—Joseph Stroud, from "As For Me I Delight in the Every
　　　Day Way" (Han Shan), in Of This World

I do not trust the gray and faithful dove.
He nests too tame, too meek a bird
when other wings lift high into the air.
Crowding the light, they rush the gentle space
of nests that are too fixed and sure.
What bird speaks best the call of love?
I do not trust the gray and faithful dove.

I have no faith in shining purple-green
where peacock tail spreads fan to catch
the sun. And surely eagles will not do,
who, wild-eyed, wheel and soar,
perching on crags that penetrate the blue.
What bird is best to tell the things we've seen?
I have no faith in shining purple-green.

No bird that sings or flies through air
will do for us the things that poets say.
Naming them all, I find no place
where tame or wild will fit the metaphor,
or give the spirit what it needs of space.
We go in love, an atmosphere more rare
than any bird that sings or climbs the air.

Part Three
Wet Weather

Between Surgeries

You ask me, Love,
if I for one brief day

could hold recovery possible,
maintain in medicine's despite

belief that you will live
and be yourself again.

This foolish faith you entertain
I try to let it in,

but hurt beyond repair
what would you have?

Let mercy keep attention
to details at hand, retrieve

in shining fragments
sharp and clear

the years we had.
For now, enough,

and everything we'd ask
to keep, to hold.

Favor

If love's final favor is forgiveness,
    it's what I want, recalling the time
we cared for a neighbor's cat
    that pushed its feeding dish off the fence
into somebody's yard. My husband said he'd go
    retrieve it, but I didn't want him getting lost,
bothering people we didn't know,
    who might not understand his speech,
confused, deliberate, slow.

    Before we die, they say we slough off layers,
become the hard bright core of who we really are,
    and he who spoke to strangers on the street as if
he'd known them always, trusted every pushy salesman
    at the door, came back with the dish in his hands,
told me it never hurts to try.

    I'm trying now, for favor:
to forgive a day I didn't trust,
    befriend the stranger-widow I've become,
remembering a white cat on the gray board fence,
    the silly flowered dish he
offered like a boy who's won the lottery,
    the dazed and tender puzzle in his eyes.

Diminuendo

How slow and dear—the words exact,
the very words—the dark came on

from rose to gray. We dozed, I think,
were safe and quiet in our minds,

went where the old songs took us, hours before
the surgeries that didn't save.

The ache in my throat says I can't write this,
can't find us in that room, the bed,

our light dry fingers all we could agree to hold,
while bittersweet in winding down of day,

Love Songs from a Chorus. And now, perhaps
another sunset's blazoned in that room, a sky

that takes some stranger by surprise, while clear and far
the singing, a dying afternoon.

Wet Weather

Tonight I track them down, slugs in the primroses, snails
in the hyacinths. Even before their sweet bells open
chewed to slippery brown nubs. I cut the slugs in half,
harvest baby snails off the chrysanthemums, collect
heavy shells in a plastic bag, crunch them all underfoot,
empty this slaughter in the compost. Trying to save the vegetables.
The fog's in, somewhere a dog won't stop barking. In our house
you're dying, going out of yourself, leaving this world.
When we say God to one another, I don't know who God is.
I decide against the snails and slugs, but they keep on,
greedy for hyacinth and lettuce. From the other side
of a gate she's too small to open, a child's crying. She
can't get back to her world of yard and toys, her house.
Outside the circle of my flashlight, the snails
leave silver lines, patterns in the dirt. Outdoors
in this dripping weather, a knife in my hand,
wet plastic sticking to itself in slime and bits of shell,
I want the child's mother here, her words
answering like God for both of us:
"It's all right now. Didn't you know I'd come?"

Difficult Work

Now your life is done, complete,
silence is the trade you ply,
your skills improving with each year
that under earth you lie.

The occupation seems to suit,
work you do alone,
without benefit of wages
contracted to a stone.

You do the job surpassing well,
I had not thought you would,
who hoped for smallest failure,
some lapse I could applaud.

New Widow Hears the Story As If For the First Time

Isis gathered the thirteen fragments of the dead king's body,
collected him piece by piece
from the gardens of white and purple agapanthus,
from under stone and sand,
out of the river's reeds.

She fastened him together,
eased his new-joined edges
with herbs and honey,
mourned
his missing part
in the claws of the crab.

On the royal barge
Isis brought Osiris home.
He was deaf to the music of flutes,
sightless before the divine images,
his travels come to this slow journey.

When the queen lay down
on the body of the dead king,
her own body opened
receptive as earth, ready
to take in rain,
the new god conceived
in miraculous white milk.

Out of long marriage
memory dreamed a son,
love's power
reviving the seed.

Boots

Before first light the widow
strikes wet wood until fire

takes hold. She bakes her bread
in a blackened oven, finds

luck in her warming bones, her life
worth more than anybody says.

Under the iron bed the worm's at work
in her husband's boots, those two

curled and hardened tongues, laces slack
in the holes. What pulls at her gut is hunger.

This Year, and the Year After

So as to pay careful attention to odd scraps of paper
So as to go into your closet and give away what is there
So as to lie down on our bed trusting your hand will find me
So as to celebrate your recorded voice in the house
     and be thankful
So as to walk under redwoods and have you
     walking beside me
So as to look through the blur of the hills and see them
     resume their original shape
So as to forgive the unawareness of lovers still able
     to touch each other
So as to speak the agony of your long dying and not
     be sentimental
So as to say it is early to talk of courage
So as to test the difficult language of sorrow and use it
So as to listen to my heart in its rhythm of changes
So as to be broken by the separation of new beginnings
So as to find a place for this song and give it a name
I am learning to sing. So as to be and become I am
     learning to sing.

Joy to the World

Reading in this morning's paper
how Isaac Watts turned Psalm 98
into this carol, I am pushed back
to the season of your dying. We
stood in the unlit hallway of our
San Francisco house, held each other
to sing against the night, my voice
wobbly, off-key, yours clear as always,
stronger. Both of us without hope
except for the song, and the years
in our arms. After the surgeries,
the prognosis, the carol heard as if
for the first time, the streets
thick with fog, colored lights
on the dark green tree.

Boundaries

A week before the last surgery,
clearing the desk as if you knew
something I didn't, you set aside
your dream journals for the trash.
It's hard to let them go, you said,
but I won't read them again.
You can have them, if you want.

Written in shorthand I couldn't read,
I kept them, nonetheless, as for years
I saved the letters, keepsakes, love-notes,
your funny birthday cards. But the journals
were your life apart, a private world,
erotic, strange, not the mutual morning stuff
we laughed at, puzzled over.

I put the journals in a drawer,
never read those pages, Love,
didn't need or want to follow you
into old fears and fantasies. The work
was yours, to dream it through
and lock the hurt away. When you died
I let the spiral notebooks go—

into that strict and private space
we held as love between us.
Then and now.

Plainsong

woke in a foreign hotel
reached for you, then
remembered the canvas sling

and men I didn't know
taking your body down the steps
too early for anyone to see,

knew you died years before,
heard whistling outside
saw light on the wings of a bird.

Elegies Beside Water

1. Trinity River
Sunlight, and September an old heart-song
alive with recollection: solace in water sound,
an absence beside the river
where mountain lilac in spring
made blue the coastal hills, the evening air
fragrant and sweet where I stand
fishing the calm, bright pools with you.

2. Creekside Nature Trail
The small ripples speak of you,
ivy climbing the ravine,
and the great downed trees
green and thick with moss.

Astonishing, this unfamiliar place
claims us. I hold onto the bridge railing,
look down. My throat tightens,
my stomach knots with old grief,
and I listen long
where there are no words.

Words do not, will not
bring you back. I have
squandered many,
and in their time they
made good enough songs,

but here is your voice
I did not expect,
clear as water over stones,
rounding and pushing the pebbles.

Meditation Rock, Appalachia

Like foxfire with no glow of its own
or sun-gleam off the wing of a Carolina raptor
wheeling the blue ridges that fog
pours through and lifts
to uncover range on mountain range,
more stones and ledges,
rocks older than the pyramids,
strata with no fossils,

you shine, your face
reflected in standing water
that gives back the sky.

You shadow my walks
through hardwoods, bunch-berry,
sweetbush, accompany me
across lowlands with almost hidden flowers:
white violet, yellow star-grass,
dog-hobble.

Between miles of green valleys
with rainfall building in the clouds
and the hawks circling,
you live in the highland gaps,
your absence
the shifting border between.

Garland of Spring Months

For March I give you kites, light as
the balsa-wood boxes you made with your Dad,
green dragons with long tails, big-winged butterflies
coasting over Marina Green. And I give you
that milk-carton boat, work of your last days,
the launching in the backyard pool
with grandchildren shouting delight.

For April I give you my girlish laughter
and my golden tears, Hilda Conkling's song
of mixed weather that says we're young again,
as I still think that we are. This is the month
I give you primroses, new varieties
from Shadow Creek Nursery, and white hyacinths,
orange tulips, the names of roses, my plans
for island travel without you, stones I bring
from the beach, stories at night and you, listening.
And stars. If heaven is dark, I am prodigal.
I give you constellations.

For May, the bright exalted morning
of your going, the early hour you left your body
that was like no other. You may not wish it back.
I give you all unfinished work,
your life after this life
I cannot, but have to, imagine.

A Place to Live

Even though—both of us knowing you could die any time,
both of us *wanting* to believe when you said this would be
the place you'd come to if you could—I seldom
come here and wait on this log that's turned almost into stone.
Even though keeping our word was life between us, given
all *that* in trust, still I seldom walk under these trees,
redwood and eucalyptus, the branches of Monterey pine
over the path opening farther than we could see the morning
you told me you'd surely try to come. I've tried being here,
stopped and stood quiet to see if you could make it, but I'm
either too early or too late and just miss you, in time
only for a voice that tells me living my life's a way of being
faithful. Even though the trees keep changing and love is
behind or ahead of me in the clearing I trust as I trust
this ground: the duff and dark needles underfoot, the light
through high green lace pulling the trees into the sky.

Part Four

His Body in the World

His Body in the World

That he should live again
That death be not oblivion
     —Gregory Orr

As if words could be his body,
the flat planes of photographs,
music he took for shelter,
his voice that shelters me now.

As if the food we ate
in the time of lament
could feed me,
and sometimes it does.

As if setting words in order
could return us to that time,
and to one another
in the years of happiness,
and almost, they do.

———

Since *after* is very cool and still
and how together we were

is for time to tell, I
tell you this, far partner,

listener in the air
and not able ever

to answer: I have
come to rely

on the heart's necessity
holding us as sunlight
holds the fields in summer,
the autumn leaves

—

October, the last plums
softening into the orchard grass,
and speckled with mold

I step warily, toss
the split and bruised fruit
to the base of the tree
that has this year been so lavish
and heavy with harvest

The plums are only one part
of the softening body of the world
I don't want to lose or leave,
and my boots have purple skins
glued to their cleated soles,
sticky remains of yellow pulp
walking me out of the field

—

When I said *gone,* I didn't believe,
though it was so.
When I said *not really,*
I juggled blue and red balls
I couldn't catch.

When I said *hope,*
the word had no luster,
no shining clothes.

—

So I stopped using abstractions
and sent them back
into the pages of my dictionary
where they are at home among concepts.

But when I say *you*
the poem knows exactly
who I mean.

—

Where did your love go,
how did you carry it
all the way past death
that never yet has stopped
the voice of the poem's
unsayable grief?

—

To be lifted on wings,
or better, to be held
in human arms and carried
to the place the poem knows.

To have the beloved bringing food
when what is set before me
burns my tongue and is bitter
in my mouth.

This is wanting
so deep no poem
can fill the ache of it.

When I say this
I kneel down
in a long shadow

—

Why don't I stop
adding words to the world?
Why doesn't the rain
stop falling? Already
the earth is saturated
and rivers flood their banks.

Too many words.
Why don't I stop?

—

For the journey out of loss
I need the lantern of the poem
swinging beside me in the dark.

—

Don't you hear him laughing?
Don't you hear his songs
waiting for you
to sing them?

Which is to say
there are poems
that want to be
the new music of his life,
stories to help him live.

Part Five

Living Alone

From Here

for all that has been, thanks
for all that shall be, yes
      —Dag Hammarskjöld, Markings

No one who looks back is fit, the gospel says,
for the kingdom. Renouncing my small hope

of getting in, disqualified by all that turns me round
in thanks for grace or chance that led me here,

I can't see where's the harm. So far I've not
been changed to salt and am no pillar in the road,

so far the winter breaks to sounds of streams ahead.
The past is iron and roses, health and sickness

as in a marriage vow. I'm pledged to all that was,
and to this moment's breath, the next.

Talking to the Dark

As if they hadn't heard it all before,
last night I told the stars who's missing
from my life, said I know it's foolish
poking at thistles, the dry stalks
crumbling to touch in a dead garden
with locked gates. Telling the stars
was relief of sorts. Out of doors
in the wide abundant night,
with the planets securely in place,
from my front porch I talked
to the stars, said thanks
for their not hearing,
and for clouds hiding the moon,
the far cold light.

Constellations

Five years, and I begin
to live easier in the world without you,
as if you're alive in the house,
reading perhaps, upstairs,
or straightening tools in the basement,
sorting the small glass jars of nails and screws,
hinges with dust in the holes.

I don't understand
this surprising new assurance,
the sky turning familiar
as when I was a child
watching and watching,
believing I was part of emptiness and space,
the cloud-shapes drifting into animals
and disappearing, the constellations
far away as legend.

Discarding the mask of your changes
I can almost remember your face.

Rosemary

Pruning the dark green spikes,
shaping the overgrown bush
to manageable form, I
cut the lopsided arms,
make room for lemon thyme
and lavender.

Between my breasts a broken sprig
sharp as grief remembered,
bruises my skin. The smell of rosemary
assaults me in the sun
and I do not want to go indoors
or change my clothes.

For Sale

I surrender, cede the territory
to strangers tramping through,
give in to the invasion. Potential buyers
take over, and I suffer their inspections
as they open closets and doors,
try the heft of the windows,
presume to measure our space.

I don't know who will come and stay,
be taken in by the new garden,
the double garage, the high ceilings
and clean walls, the light
shifting between the rooms
as it does hour by hour.

But when escrow is in place,
the papers signed and keys
handed over, they will not know
how steadily we stay married here.

Their deed gives no title
to consciousness alive in these rooms,
the secret life in the grain of the floors.

Who comes to live here after us
has to bring their own gods.

New Owners Paint the House

Old color will surface, show through cream,
through new paint. Deep blue does that,

lines under brush strokes that don't quite
cover our traces, the days we spent

matching and choosing, holding cardboard
swatches of color next to the front door,

the window-trim, comparing combinations,
crossing the street to check appearances:

Solitude Blue and *Moby Dick, Whisper White*
we wanted to erase a pale, insipid green.

Neighbors say the new colors are elegant,
Mediterranean. I say our house stays blue

as the sea is blue, bold as New England coastline,
memory's high-masted sloop riding out the weather

in widening circles of foam into blue
that crests and breaks, does not go under.

Threshold

Walking the bridge over the tide flats,
looking as far as I can, the Narrows
run to open water, on and on the way you
said the ocean does when you looked to the Pacific
at the end of your life.

Two gulls wade the mud, others
take off in winter weather. Sailboats
ride anchor at the pier, masts swaying
in the wet air. Overcast and gray
this northern sky is not California,
but I will live my seasons under it.

I want to tell you I left our house,
made a smaller nest. I want you
to say it's all right
to let go of things,
live with essentials.

You did, took time
for words you said I might need.
(Like food. Like light.)

Turning the new key in an unfamiliar door
I tell you we cross the threshold together,
find rooms proportioned to love's work,
the comely symmetry of change.

Living Alone

I miss you in unlikely things: this afternoon
    a green recycling cart
heavy as my envy for women whose partners
    push bins to the street
and point the arrows right for pick-up.
    You bundled newspapers,
tied them square, set the garbage out,
    at night turned down
the thermostat. Living alone, I forget,
    wake up in a room too warm.
Today's huge and uncomposted lump
    is my need to talk with you,
(not *to*, but *with* you, Love) about our angry son.
    I haven't found a way
to help him break this jam, and he's a powder keg
    set to explode, problems on the job
testing him to the limit. Stubborn, proud as you,
    this boy become a man,
he finds it hard to ask for help. I'm learning
    to ask: how to replace batteries
in the garage door-opener, smoke detector,
    change the furnace filter,
balance the checkbook, do taxes, gas up the car.
    I thought I'd done it right,
forgiving you as dead for being dead, and can be
    glad for crocus in the grass, tulips,
yellow dandelions, these roiling skies of March,
    day's light announcing change. I thought
I'd taken on my widow's life. Although I'm here,
    and have to be the one he calls, I know I can't
be father to his hurt, his need, though your loud silence
    asks for this, and more
from days I'm learning slowly to forgive.

Warm Night in August

summer lust is in me
and what am I to do with my bare skin

so alive I want you not less
for that life behind us

if my shadow falls in love
who runs with her when the sun

boils honey in the sky, the wind
mean as parting, rust on my tongue

how will I sleep
under a drunken moon

watch over me, rain,
rock my ship to the sea

Who I Mean to Be

You seem to grow stronger
and more playful as memory
runs back into shadow.

Who I mean to be to you now
I have no language for,
having exhausted words,
poems made from grief and love.

Who I mean to be is
nothing added to that life,
everything I was and was not,
music that finds you gone.

I mean to be
that wild soft tongue,
a solitary animal
that licks its paws and hunkers down
to sleep on your grave.

Slow Time

We'll be in our boat on the river,
drifting along on a summer day.

We won't be pulling the oars. I'll
watch leaf-shadows on your back,

and not want to keep any of this:
the green water, our not talking.

Later, we'll go uphill to the old barn,
roll in the hay, sleep for a long time.

You won't be dying, and the children
haven't been born. I won't be looking

for the missing half of my life.

Going Back to the Farm: Two Poems

One
I thought there would be a new ceremony of words
in this familiar place, but I didn't even make it
to the upper field and the rock cairn.
This time I didn't dream of you
with me on that rain-washed road.

I'd like to write something new,
a few words maybe for the black spider
on the white door, or the Japanese beetles
and box elder bugs crawling up my bed sheets at night.
The insects at least are real,
as the rattle and tick
of dry pods and stalks are real,
the last sounds of summer,
a scent of fall in the air.

If you could say anything about this, you might
rather have a poem for the dead fly on the window sill,
or one for the spotted ladybug at my wrist.
No further elegy of loss. If you're listening,
maybe you'd rather hear the clink of glasses
raised to the ancestors, our chairs scraping the floor
when we pull up to the table. Maybe you'd rather
not be reminded of when you sat here
gaunt and ill, counting out the medicines
that never could make you well. I suspect you'd
prefer hearing young Tolliver who told me
"You walk pretty good," his warning
about the slippery steps after last night's rain.

Two

On the wet skylight, yellow leaves.
Knot-holes open eyes in the door frame.

Walking stick, a third foot for grandmother.
Uphill, to a grave in the orchard.

The shine in the fields is presence, is absence.
Indications are that neither lasts long.

Red-winged blackbirds fly over the reeds.
We look for the memory in water.

I don't see the river that you see.
That the river is there makes a difference.

Making the drum is the first drumbeat.
Between hand-skin and hide-skin, the ancestors.

They come with the light behind them.
In the next room, sounds of nobody there.

Without

I had not thought to trust the cobalt curtain
or the chilly tile, and not my feet upon the orange floor,
or planned to give the slightest happy token
to the day. The sun's red line enough,
that it should fall across the space his body made,
the slatted light enough, the shining panes
that turn in time to gold. That he should lie so still
and sleep so long while I, alive in bright September air
have eyes too cold for tears, my empty hands
too aching cold, that tend a dying fire.

October Dreams

Nights and days follow me into autumn,
drop like leaves from the emptying trees
that make way for light. Like the leaves,
I am called toward earth, toward home,
and home is any place you are.

We move toward and away from each other,
hungry, wanting more.

The dark asks questions,
brings brain-cinema dreams,
sometimes a sweet replay,
or nightmare that shivers me awake.

Each arousal accompanies me into daylight,
sends me out of doors
where I stand missing you
under the brilliant fall of leaves,
hold my arms to the sky.

First Light in Winter: a Meditation

I.

Winter mornings start slow,
my mouth dry as a snake's,
body stumbling from sleep,
holding onto phantasms
out of the old reptilian brain.

Don't wake too soon, I say,
tell myself it's time
to stay where I am,
a shell in tidal water,
the dark ocean pulling me in.

Gradually the heat comes on,
my body stirs, warms

and I remember
a starling at the seed-heart
of the bare crabapple tree,
a question: which is the tree,
that skeleton, or
summer's green
in full leaf?

Outside the bedroom window
a chill rose-lemon sunrise.

2.

Settling my heart into winter
I have put the garden to bed.

Watch over us, sky,
blow through me, time,
show the diamond glint
in the icy sidewalk,
sing the stars to sleep.

Let the black ships go under
where the fingers of light
are drowning in turbulent water,
my one love no more with me
bare and sweet as summer rain.

Winter cries on my tongue.
What I want is to chant the sun nearer,
shape frozen language into music,
be drunk if that's what winter asks,
the wind mean as parting.
You gone. Me here.

3.

In this gray season of comings and goings,
the daily reports of new deaths
in the chill hours of early morning.
Sometimes after long suffering
an easy slipping away. Memory falls
like an old coat off the hanger.

And the newborn slide into life
with a slap on the rump to get them going.

I am thinking also of poetry,
the eloquence of stories that take me
all the way to the cold horizon
where I see you walking in the stiff stubble
of freezing hay-fields.

Although I can almost hear you
singing, your boots make no prints
on the ground, the falling snow
a curtain of light I can't
pull apart, or see through.

Endearments

I only borrowed these words,
and you may have them back.

Arrange them as you will,
I did my best to shape them

into pleasing combinations
dancing side by side.

But in my hot and secret heart
love is the one and only word.

These others I have borrowed
steal luster from the sun.

Beside the Dosewallips River

It was a morning of river music,
the same river that sang all night
in and under my dreams, moving
my hands toward your body, and I
forgot everything I ever learned except
our love-times. I forgot everything
I can never tell you. The river carried me
on its back and now it seems I am towing it,
testing the ground along the bank with my stick,
through knee-high ferns and the downed trees.
An unknown bird is romping on the rocks,
and all the while the river is rushing and going,
music that can only be towed by the heart
into the morning of one particular day, this one
that is here and shining, and forever now.

Acknowledgments

My thanks to the editors of journals where these poems appeared:

Barnwood: "Beside the Dosewallips River," "Plainsong."
Buffalo Spree: "Constellations," "Rosemary." An early version of "For
    Sale" was published as "Selling the House."
Christian Science Monitor: "New Owners Paint the House."
4th Street: "Yes, there is."
Friends Bulletin: "On Saving the World."
Georgetown Review: "Without."
Hawaii Review: "Shell Beach."
The Lyric: "Covenant," "Jealous Woman Weaving."
Manzanita Quarterly: "New Widow Hears the Story As If For the First
    Time."
The Mennonite: "From Here," "Joy to the World."
Nimrod: "First Light in Winter: A Meditation," "Living Alone."
Raven Chronicles: "Threshold."
Santa Clara Review: "Long Day, and the Child Asleep."
Search (National Brain Tumor Foundation): "This Year, and the Year
    After."
Snow Monkey: "Beginning Autumn."
Wellspring: "What I Need to Hear."
White Pelican: "Talking to the Dark."

"A Place to Live," and "For New Lovers in North Country" are
reprinted from *Granite Under Water*; "Sidewalk Café" from *Flying
Horses*; and "How Could You Not" from *The Light of Invisible Bod-
ies* (all from John Daniel & Co.). "Wet Weather" first appeared in
Between Silence and Answer (Pendle Hill, 1994). Several poems are
from *Greatest Hits 1956-2000*, a Pudding House chapbook. "Passage"
was published in *Where the Field Goes* (1976) and reprinted in *Thread
That Sings in My Hands*, winner of the 2004 National Looking Glass

chapbook award from Pudding House. Other poems are from out-of-print collections.

Part two of "Returning to the Farm" was published as "Ghazal: Bubbling Springs Farm" in the 2004 chapbook *Strange Familiars* (New Market Press).

"His Body in the World," the lyric sequence of Part Four, owes a debt to Gregory Orr's *Concerning the Book That Is The Body Of The Beloved,* published by Copper Canyon Press.

The book's opening epigraph is from Stephen Mitchell's translation *The Selected Poetry of Rainer Maria Rilke* (Random House)